$\updownarrow$ LEGAL $\longleftrightarrow$ DAISY $\longleftrightarrow$ SPACING $\updownarrow$

LEGAL DAISY SPACING

The *BUILD-A-PLANET* Manual
of Official World Improvements

CHRISTOPHER WINN

RANDOM HOUSE
NEW YORK

For my wife Sheridan

Copyright © 1985 by Christopher Winn

All rights reserved under International and Pan-American
Copyright Conventions. Published in the United States by
Random House, Inc., New York. Originally
published in Great Britain by William Heinemann Ltd., London.

Library of Congress Cataloging in Publication Data

Winn, Christopher.
  Legal daisy spacing.
  1. Environmental protection—Caricatures and
cartoons. 2. English wit and humor, Pictorial.
  I. Title.
  NC1479.W53A4 1985   741.5'942   85-2329
  ISBN 0-394-74157-9

Manufactured in Great Britain
First edition 24689753

CONTENTS

FOREWORD

←⎯⎯ ⎯⎯→

by
The Chairman, Build-A-Planet

Friends! This little book is put into your hands in the sincere hope that the study and observance of its provisions will make your planet a safer, more hygienic, a finer place to live.

As we all know, our happy Universe was once a rough untidy sort of place, a senseless muddle of unruly orbs, a chaos of uncharted spaces, a swollen parcel of sulky gases and pustular spheres. Luckily today we are mostly free of such disorderliness. That subversive Spirit of Nature which runs through all things with abandoned zeal is now checked and monitored daily. Never before have we enjoyed such levels of hygiene, comfort and order as now exist in the modern Universe: meter-controlled radiance schedules have solved the problem of unlawful sunshine (suns throughout the Charted Heavens now behave with suitable discretion); Black Hole evacuation programmes go like clockwork (thanks to recent advances in suppositorial technology); the official Netting of Stray Comets is proving fruitful; organized level-belpering and vimblicous Boodle-Drives are just around the corner; and the Boldergrab is on the drawing-board!

But be not deceived into idleness! There is still much work to be done — labour for the Handyman! Always be on guard during your improvement schemes; keep notes, and report all irregularities on the appropriate forms. Expect subversive vegetation, running water and vile clouds. Expect bipedal growths and the Deciduous Tree. Cairn all mountains; lubricate all shores; restrain all menhirs; purify all waters. These are the rules. Keep them bright upon your hearts and experiment tirelessly within the sanction of the Law. Have courage, and remember: Order through Vigilance, Decency through Purification.

Belem C. Plentile

EMBELEN
DRIAND
NAY BODRING
ZWOLL

← 1 →
PREPARING
THE
SURFACE

Let smoothness be your byword! The surface of the modern planet should be smooth and regular, glossy and highly light-reflecting. Direct all your attentions to this end. Acquaint yourself with the pustularity of the spheres: it is the sad truth that most unattended planets suffer from severe crust problems. Reckless spinning in unauthorized orbits stirs up all manner of wicked venoms, which rise up through the crust and burst forth with odious vigour on the surface. As time goes by these malodorous excrescences solidify to form hazardous surface features: treacherous mountains, peaks and crags, where gather dribbly clouds that feed the scurrilous streams and unpredictable seas; valleys deep with loose and riotous greenery, the hiding-place of delinquent lakes and disgraceful self-exposing waterfalls; canyons, the lairs of sinuous rivers; and coasts, haphazard with unhealthy cliffs, impertinent peninsulars and the barrage of the disrespectful tides. Learn then to recognise the woeful signs of planetary neglect: look to your Gradaplax, and go!

Levelling with the Gradaplax

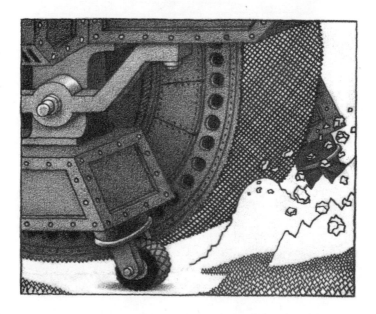

Make short work of irregular and dangerous surface features with Krolz's Auxiliary Rustless Gradaplax. Recommended for all crust problems in a recent report of the Select Committee for Rationalizing Planetary Excavations (SCRAPE).

Ocean Draining

Good ocean maintenance requires proper draining. Scour round all those edges and scrub that bottom well! Add plenty of disinfectant to the water as you refill to prevent the growth of harmful marine life.

Removing Mould

Mould is unsightly and can cause much damage to the surface of the modern Countryside. Flick off neatly with a trowel and cover the area with sterile material. Now wash your hands.

Stubborn Outcrops

The Serious Handyman will always keep a set of humble crag files ready for tackling those obstinate little jobs. Especially handy when the Gradaplax is away on weightier business. Be resourceful!

Easy Ravine Fillers

These ugly gashes should be filled without delay. Start at the bottom (dark and smelly!), squeeze out filler and work right up to the top. Sand off for a smooth finish.

Jungle Flooring

The very latest jungle floorcoverings come in a huge range of fashionable colours and patterns. No need for underlay — just clear and lay in one smooth operation with Automatic Greenery Sweepers.

17

Slope Tagging

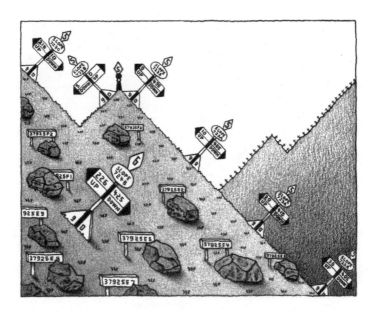

Slopes are dangerous places and must be tagged at once. Use only Official Slope Tags. You should also record all rocks, pebbles and plivets. This is in accordance with Bureau of Statistical Boulderation Requirement 27b.

Smartening Cliffs

Smart cliffs are healthy cliffs! Tap away loose material with a chisel. Now you are ready to apply your cement and lay on the Washable Coastline Tiles.

Smooth Dune Moving

Shifting sands are a messy business and spread anarchy and confusion. Regular armed patrols in motorized dunes will soon sort out any disorderly activity. Work by night and in pairs.

Standard Iceberg Moulds

Standardize your icebergs! The new Series 22 Official Standard Iceberg represents the latest development in Pre-formed Iceberg Technology and is unbreakable, unsinkable and unmeltable.

21

← 2 →
DEALING
WITH
GREENERY

←——————→

Wilful are the ways of the Countryside, and enthusiastic the eruptions of unsupervised greenery. Establish at the outset a systematic programme of vegetation control. Those minor floral disobediences may be dealt with easily using the Spoiling Cabinet, but the higher greeneries will require a more sophisticated approach. Beware particularly the Deciduous Tree! This gross unwieldy structure is characterized by an abandoned globosity of form, a random and unhealthy distribution of limbs, and an inner nature of the most degenerate kind. In addition it has a particularly unpleasant habit of shedding its leaves every year. These make for clutter, will clog up machinery, and can seriously disturb those glistening surfaces you are striving to achieve. Recent night-time tests indicate that the Deciduous Tree can move about from place to place under cover of darkness. This surprising fact has been suspected for some while, and in regularized plantations of normal healthy conifers a stray Deciduous Tree can spread corruption virtually overnight. In spite of this, normal wrenching techniques may prove inadequate — the Deciduous Tree holds the ground with an obstinacy unique among the greeneries.

Fixing Pre-Greased Crotoplates

For small greenery jobs nothing is as effective as the Pre-Greased Crotoplate. Just clamp the unit down and set the timer! The very best crotogrease is made from grodules of Stogging Lime.

The Willerby Fluzopositor

The Willerby Fluzopositor delivers a handy punitive dose of 60zds of Fluzopiltric Acid to the wayward root systems of the lower greeneries. It is silent, automatic, and works tirelessly day and night.

Cactus Thimbling

Beware the prongs of desert greeneries! These Grade 1 Approved Cactus Thimbles are quality products and have been shown in recent Prickle Tunnel tests to withstand levels of up to 93.25owz.

A Portable Rock Garden

A portable rock garden is the ideal, discreet housing for your Spoiling Cabinet (see Appendix 1 for a list of suggested contents). Fluff up the plants once in a while for that spring freshness.

Routine Mushroom Surveillance

Exceptional vigilance is necessary in the matter of mushrooms – down among the rotting leaves subversion thrives. Use the latest ultra-sensitive MushroMonitors to pick up the least whisper of fungal conspiracy.

A Hanging Garden

This handy Floral Disobedience Enclosure Unit will serve you well for many years. Using one of the new withering agents, you can even fit a shrub or fruiting bush into your arrangement.

Isolating the Intruder

Sometimes, in the dead of night, a Deciduous Tree will get into a plantation of normal healthy conifers. O shame! O degradation! Detain in a well-lit compound before beginning corrective therapy.

Untidy Vegetation

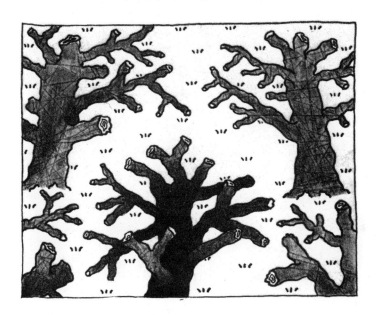

Proper decidual discipline requires the removal of dangerous lurking greenery. A set of No.5 tree snippers should do the job. Remember to take unwanted wildlife home with you.

31

Successful Tree Coning

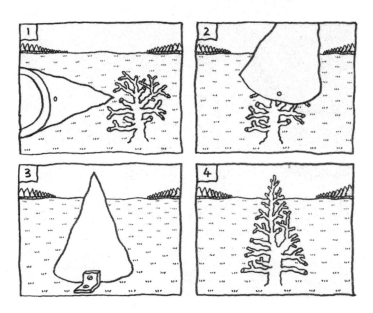

Tree coning can be tricky, and few conversions are wholly successful. This is due, it is thought, to the barbarous nature of Deciduous Trees. Your equipment should be serviced regularly by reputable cone operatives.

A Forest Pontoon

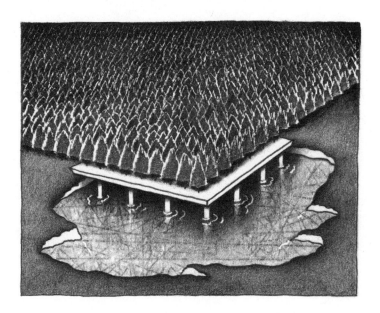

The three 'R's of Essential Forest Symmetry are: Right-angles, Rulers and Wriddle-jillets. Asymmetric coniferation is an offence punishable by law. Prepare your pontoons!

3
A WORD
ABOUT
WATER

Keep your rivers and seas, your lakes and pools free from clear running water. Fresh water is the very life-blood of anarchy and subversion: invisible, mysterious, fugitive and fickle, it is an affront to order and stability, to decency and truth. It is the succour of Bipedal Growths (see Chapter 7), the draught of Lichens, the cursed tipple of Deciduous Trees.

Pursue running water without pity or fatigue, and trap it with determination. Attend to its purification with thoroughness and zeal. Transport it only in officially registered plumbous receptacles. Dispose of it only in authorized underground dumps. Do not underestimate the power of clear running water! Be stout of heart and handle it with care: not all water loses its dangerous motile energy when collected. Therefore secure properly the tops of your receptacles during transportation. Remember: Order through Vigilance, Decency through Purification!

Official Plumbous Receptacles

Dangerous running water should be carried only in properly registered Official Plumbous Receptacles. It is a sensible precaution to travel by night in order to minimize the possibility of local objection.

Geyser Sheaths

Geysers are excitable by nature and throw shameless jets of hot water high into the air at the least provocation. These disgraceful eruptions must be contained at once by fitting pre-stressed Geyser Sheaths.

Atoll Management

Atoll water should not be allowed to stay clear. It is well worth the trouble putting in a good soiling unit like this Squalorette to keep it murky. Ranch-style fencing adds a homely touch.

Flying Lakes

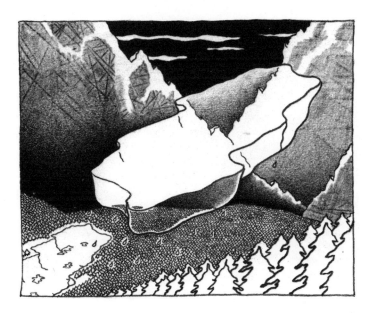

It is a little-known fact that lakes may take flight from their beds during the summer. This is strictly a matter for the Hydropolice, who are trained to deal with such an emergency.

Tidal Znidgits

Tides need a firm hand, and what better than to use a Znidgit like the Willerby 90 shown here. These characterful devices have quickly become welcome features of the coastline.

Waterfall Security

This charming scheme proves that security need not be at the expense of comfort. Piped waterfalls reduce noise! Indeed, experts using babble-meters have found that noise levels near these waterfalls are virtually zero.

4
STRUCTURAL
PROBLEMS

From time to time in the course of your improvements you may come across strange mineral concretions deposited on the surface of the Countryside. These ugly assemblages of stonework or metal remain a complete mystery, and even the most careful analysis by x-ray diffraction has been unable to give a hint as to their origin or purpose.

Some experts suggest that they might be the result of unidentified gravitational pressures. Others believe that they might be the work of primitive biological forces. Whichever the case, they are often dangerously unstable in structure and wilfully subversive in form. There is even evidence to suggest that in common with Deciduous Trees (see Chapter 2) they have the power to move about from place to place under cover of darkness.

Needless to say, a programme of regular and meticulous surveillance is called for. Whenever possible, restrain with harnesses or chafing rods. Where stricter measures are required, handle with care and destroy with ferocity.

Dealing with Piers

These rickety old structures are a menace. You'll find the timber is usually rotten and can be sawn through with ease. File down the stumps for a clean finish.

Bothersome Bridges

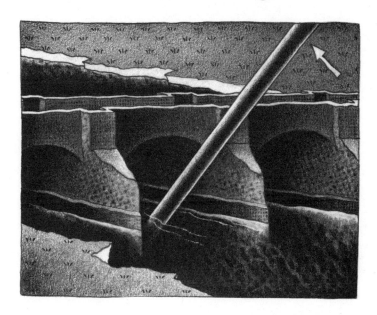

Here's a job for a nice day out. Uproot with a stout iron bar — your bridge should come away cleanly in one piece. Pound remaining stonework firmly into river-bed.

Laminating Pyramids

Pyramids are old and mysterious and require a firm hygienic coating to prevent the mystery escaping. Modern pyramid laminates come in a variety of colours and textures: illustrated is Autumn Hessian Mid Sand 22.

Obelisk Precautions

Most obelisks will snap off at the base if given a good push. The Universal Auto-Mandibles will cope with the heavy rubble – leftovers should be treated with Spoiling Powder No. 7 and buried in sterilized canisters.

47

Lancing Sudden Castles

Deal swiftly with all strange outbursts of masonry. Swab affected area well, then burst the offending excrescence with your lance. Bag up debris for incineration.

A Parish Church Compressor

Do wear goggles! Modern parish church compressors exert a terrific downward thrust which sends stained glass flying in all directions. Gather the broken pieces and set into the tops of walls (see page 106).

5
WORTHWHILE
OILING
SCHEMES

The *sine qua non* of all worthwhile oiling schemes is flexibility. Be ever vigilant for those dry spots and resourceful in their lubrication. Experiment with mixtures from your Spoiling Cabinet. You will find most modern oils will enhance the surface of the Countryside, and a variety of beautiful and long-lasting effects can be achieved. The new glossy sheens look very seductive, and of course being highly light-reflecting, are a safety plus. If you want a sophisticated contemporary appearance, go for one of the latest matt finishes. Or you might like to try your hand at texturing for that homely, personalized look.

Whichever oil you decide upon, choose a scheme that is simple to run. Beginners will particularly appreciate the four-week rotation scheme to be found overleaf. This was pioneered for coastal regions, but is flexible enough to be used anywhere.

Coastal Slickwork

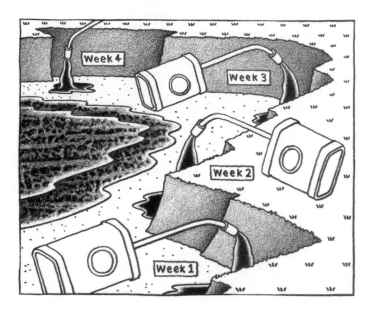

Train the jets well up into all those sly crevices. Winkle out small life-forms you may have missed. And remember: a steady rhythmic motion makes for the most even distribution.

52

The Adjustable Di-Porvulate Flowgrotniad

For regular and systematic lubrication you will
need a Flowgrotniad. This is a high-pressure
programmable multi-soiling unit with locking
bloat nuts and variable slop-troughing dribble
feeds.

Creative Lagoonery

This scheme features a new oil developed at the Institute of Creative Lagoonery. It looks like water but is actually a highly viscous soiling agent! Just right for those problem areas of untreated greenery.

Decorative Flosswork

Floss is a marvellous decorative addition to the Countryside, and comes straight from the manufacturer in a startling array of pungencies. Coastal fans will keep it airborne for many hours.

Vimblicous Wizzle-Dripping

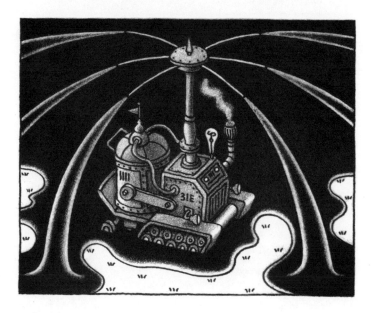

Wizzle-Dripping is endorsed by the Ancient Society of Drainmen and Lumpstoggers, and accords with Seepage Office Directive 7d.

Advanced Sog Distribution

For really efficient ground coverage you should consider sogging. In the past many sogs fell far short of desirable soiling levels, but as from this year all sogs must meet Approved Soiling Standard SG25363.

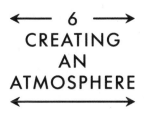

CREATING
AN
ATMOSPHERE

Learn to master the Weather, that most capricious disturber of the atmosphere. Beware of clouds, those insecure and filthy bladders of clear water, which move about upon the winds and dribble over Handiworks below. Replace your clouds with smogs, and strive for that happy state of half-light, which, withholding the full and ugly potential of the sun, will ration base and dissipated greeneries.

Maintain a stench upon the waters and the land. Be munificent with your gaseous dispensations as you were generous with your oily deployments. Search all the particles and fertile globes of Chemistry for strange pervading odours with which to concoct those rhapsodies of olfactory invention. Service all transmitters and receivers regularly and be sure to broadcast only on authorized fume wavelengths (see Appendix 2).

Do not, in your manipulations, neglect the part of noise and clatter. Coordinate your storms and refer all electrical problems to the Department of Rumblous Fulguration. Grade hail and sleet, and discipline the snowflake. Improve slush, and punish icicular disobedience. And lastly, treat the flaunting and refractory rainbow.

A Cloud Detention Centre

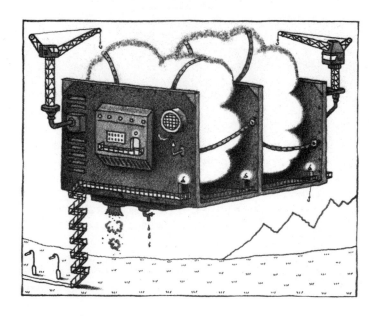

Clouds are disgustingly incontinent and most unpredictable in the shelter they provide from the harmful rays of the sun. Detain in Approved Centres. Now you are ready to bring on the smogs!

Smog Gondolas

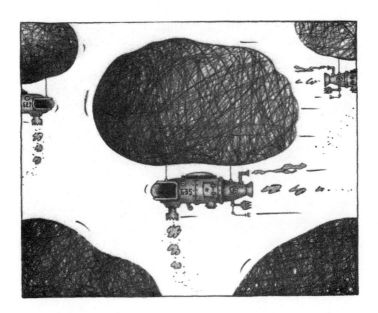

Successful smoggery depends upon mobility. The Directory of Gloominous Onubilation (available from The Smog Office) lists a wide range of high-performance smog gondolas. Shown here is the Smogster Rapide 99i.

Registered Sunlight Meters

These meters are now compulsory and are designed to detect excessive levels of sunlight in accordance with new official radiance schedules. Computers at Central Smog Control will dispatch smogs automatically to any danger area.

Installing Weazle-Jets

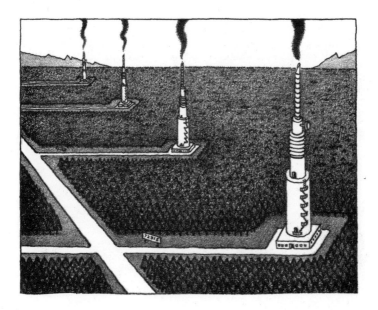

Certain tracts of land may require heavy-duty smogging, and the answer to this is synchronized Weazle-Jetting. Jets should be installed at close intervals along your major soiling squines for maximum atmospheric penetration.

63

Loud Thunderspeakers

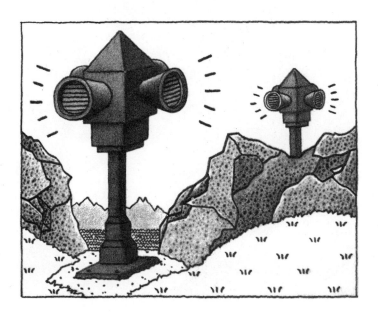

In recent trials at the Centre for Atmospheric Discord these Loud Thunderspeakers attained a meritable stridency level of 773.98 blts (Public Nuisance Factor 10). This is cause for celebration!

Broadcasting Useful Smells

Smells come very high on anybody's list of atmospheric requirements, and the Serious Handyman will be eager to make use of new developments in Stinkerative Technology. Stench broadcasting is the latest thing, and a list of frequencies is shown in Appendix 2.

A Hail Funnel

The Official Mk3 Hail Funnel is a fully mobile hail defence unit with an optional ten-speed bombardment facility. It is shown here working on maximum over a troublesome deciduous tree.

An Overnight Lightning Case

You'll find this luxury case just right for all those flashy summit jobs. It has plenty of pockets for your little extras and has been designed to take most standard makes of lightning bolt.

Modern Rainbow Bleaching

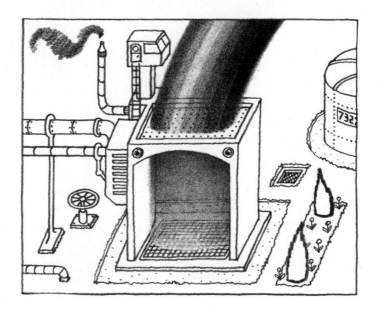

By far the best way to deal with gaudy exhibitionist displays. Bleaching comes under the jurisdiction of the Spectrum Constable, who will want to see your sterile tanks every two months.

A Mirage Trolley

Regular mirage fumigation is an essential part of desert hygiene, and the Super XE-40 makes light work of this unpleasant task. Unclog the vuple hatch from time to time.

7
CONTROLLING
PESTS

Poor pest control programmes in the past have meant that the surface of the Countryside abounds with errant Bipedal Growths. These simple life-forms are liable to gather in quite large communities under untreated slabs of masonry, and will maintain a high degree of obduracy in the face of all but the most advanced winkling procedures. The use of Puffers or other liformal abruptioning systems is a possibility, but the residual jelly may linger and cause damage to coniferous trees. Most modern regularization pro-grammes are able to offer restricted freedom to Bipedal Growths, and the rudimentary strength which these strange creatures possess can often be harnessed for undertaking simple chores around the planet. Gather in shallow trays and store in darkness.

WARNING

It cannot be emphasized too strongly: keep all Growths and other dangerous substances clearly labelled, safely packaged and under lock and key. In all cases of emergency contact The Pest Office immediately.

Winkling Procedures

The System 27 Autowinkler is perfect for the quick removal of Bipedal Growths from awkward nooks and crannies. It features powerful Willerby vibrogrippers, heat-seeking floggle tongs, and a suction maldaprode with handy drip tray.

Interview Modules

These days there are interview modules to suit all tastes. Handicap Interview Seats are now more or less standard, and the very latest modules have the sensible addition of a Chute Facility.

Using The Squapliate Flenderscales

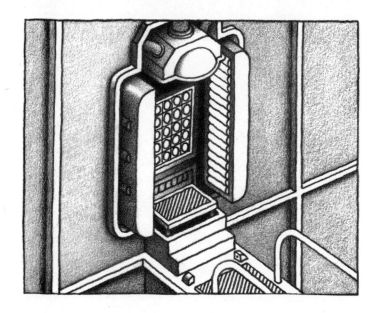

This is an authorized multi-functional grey-phased testing facility suitable for all normal sprone-graded downmeddling applications.

Disposal Chutes and Reject Bins

Disposal Operatives Manual (Section 34a) recommends a complete overhaul of the slip-beam plunge ignition system every six months, and a proper routing of the jetsam drains.

8
THE
COMMUNITY
SPIRIT

During the course of your planetary improvements you are bound to have problems with that dark, unruly wasteland that surrounds you, the Universe. The Universe was once even more disorderly than it is now — the Creation, as the records show, was a somewhat hasty affair. Fortunately we are now in the middle of Phase 1 of an extensive redevelopment scheme known as The Official Universal Modernization Programme.[1]

Once upon a time the universe was thought to be infinite, but scientists have recently discovered that this is not so.[2] Moreover, the Official Census of Heavenly Bodies has revealed that there are in fact only 22,537,261[974] million registered Bodies in the unwholesome spaces of the Universe. These are your neighbours, and this chapter advises you how to deal with some of the troublesome problems they cause.

1. For some time now the Universe and all its fixtures and fittings has been in the hands of The Nuisever Development Corporation, of which Build-A-Planet is a Licensed Subsidiary.
2. The precise dimensions of the Universe are classified information and are protected under Section 956327d of the Cosmic Secrets Act.

Attractive Stellar Grids

The night sky is a meaningless jumble of old stars, and should be screened where possible by replacement grids. Stand in rows for maximum coverage.

Replacement Galaxies

As those old-style galaxies wear out you should replace them with officially registered Galactic Units. Cheap galaxy remoulds will only cause you trouble.

Checking Comet Visas

All passes must be shown. Duty Officers are empowered under Section 92 of the Illegal Comets Act to detain any visitor found in possession of suspicious interstellar matter.

Polishing Those Rings

Some planets pick up all kinds of cosmic dust and get scruffy very quickly. Cleaning and main-tenance is handled by the Interplanetary Sanitation Authority, which will also undertake the removal of old moons.

Administering Black Hole Enemas

These irritable old heavenly bodies get badly constipated and are a continual menace to us all. A sensible evacuation programme should always include the fitting of a new Approved Black Hole Suppository.

82

Problem Sunspots

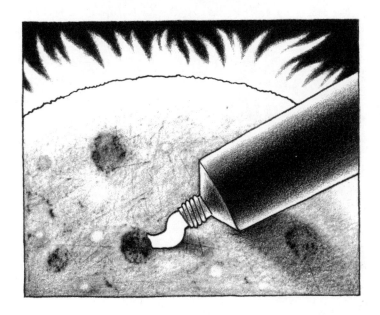

Spots may appear on the surface of your Sun from time to time. These unhealthy pustules should be squeezed out and a good solar spot cream applied to the affected area.

A Zodiac Asylum

As part of the drive towards cleaning up the night sky, committal notices have been served on several fanciful constellations. This also goes for Red Giants, White Dwarves and other fairytale nonsense.

The Plutobooster

Pluto takes 248 years to orbit the Sun. This is just not good enough. Henceforth, it has been decided, Pluto must go 10 times faster, and so a special booster has lately been fitted by technicians from Orbital Control.

9
HEALTH
AND
SAFETY

All elements within the compass of your Schemes and Handiworks should be checked and monitored daily, from the disposition of the lowest greeneries to the arrangement of the furthest stars. Mountains, menhirs, meteors, molluscs – nothing must remain beyond the bounds of your vigilance, however small. Report with speed to the relevant Superintending Authority all insubordinations, deviations and irregularities using the appropriate Form. This is the basis of a safe and healthy Universe. Never be without your Official Mobile Form Repository. The OMFR is a sophisticated, indexed Form Trolley providing constantly updated Authorized Notification Forms and up-to-the-minute comprehensive statistical documentation on every imaginable detail of interplanetary life. Additionally, it offers multi-plubricious centralized deplideration in accordance with current level 16 rating schedules. You should use your Trolley at all times to check off any irregularity you may come across. Keep it clean and always fully stocked. Never leave it unattended in mountainous regions or areas of deciduous woodland.

Dangerous Bends

Discreet signs and signals are installed in the Countryside for your well-being. You are required implicitly to conform to the indications of all signs and signals By Order.

The Dawn Patrol

Pipes and pylons need to be checked scrupulously for any irregularity that may have occurred in the night. Report all offences on Pylon Deviance Form 73256P.

Menhir Harnesses

Some standing stones have been known to creep about under cover of darkness. Round-the-clock fettering is the safe way to deal with these unpredictable structures. Chafing rods may be necessary.

Earthquake Grab Handles

Personal safety under seismic attack is uncondi-
tionally guaranteed with the Mk1 Official Grab
Handle. This has been designed to remain stable
even during tremors registering 8.9 on the
Richter Scale. Survival through Protection!

Volcano Freshening

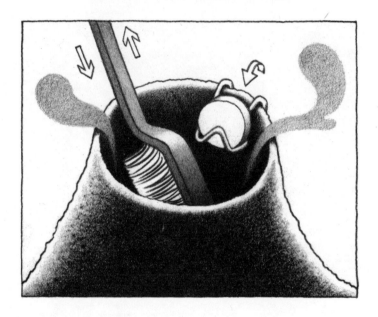

Squirt disinfectant down the bowl of your volcano every morning and scrub with a stiff brush. Hang a scented freshener over the rim for that spring freshness.

Lava Bollarding

"Lava Wardens must report any failure of the Bollard Switching Mechanisms immediately to the Chief Volcanic Superintendent at Operational Traffic Control." — Section 932b, The Volcano Code.

Handy Tree Screens

Uphold the Laws of Decency at all times and keep those deciduous trees well covered. Handy tree screens can be obtained in a wide variety of sympathetic finishes like this attractive leatherette.

Meteor Trampolines

Special trampolines have been installed to protect the Countryside from the menace of meteor bombardment. Re-springing should only be undertaken by authorized technicians from the Meteor Defence Commission.

95

Surplus Island Storage

Make sure you tidy up your spare islands at the end of the day. They must not be left floating around overnight where they might knock into newly decorated coastlines.

A Mollusc Prison

The Mollusc Prison has been designed to strike terror into the hearts of these vicious and deplorable creatures. Compulsory molluscration is the latest in a long line of creative reforms from Marine Security.

Cairning Procedures

All mountain summits must be cairned without delay. Secure the Plivet Stone on each cairn, then wheel the finished structure to the summit. This will be found at the end of the uphill slope.

Lighting the Countryside

Carefully planned lighting will greatly enhance the appearance of your Countryside, especially if you fit the new Luride filters. These offer a variety of attractive scenic effects from Apricot Sunset to Chartreuse Neon Dawn.

Tornado Bottling

Tornadoes and hurricanes can be stored quite safely in approved jars and make excellent abrasive tools for those tricky crust jobs. More unruly hurricanes can be pinned to the ground through the eye before bottling.

Sturdy Avalanche Bins

These sturdy bins are essential in mountain areas where there is a danger from falling snow. Snow will be collected for processing by Avalanche Operatives every Monday.

No-Snowing Zones

Unscheduled winter settling is an annual problem and can cause great damage to smogs and Oiling Schemes. Snow control is now in the hands of the Special Precipitations Executive.

Authorized Glacier Barriers

Glaciers are sneaky and will creep up on you unawares. Your barriers should be of stout construction and fixed firmly to the ground. Size 8 screws should do the job.

Now that your overall development scheme is well under way you may like to consider one or two extra touches for the imaginative enhancement of your planetary environment. These decorative building projects are but a small selection from the Build-A-Planet Masterfile, an enormous and expanding project reference system which is open to all Serious Handymen.

And the future? Tests are even now being run with a prototype Boldergrab, although the frequency of flux pulsation in the droning blades is still a little worrying. There is Adhesive Moth Dusting to look forward to, currently in the research stage; there is Rain Staining, a new approved Monument Wrench, Orbital Braking Pads, a Meadow Spade, De-spiralous Nebulation, Rotating Flint Dispatch, Yellow Dripe Towers and New Moon Registration; there is a fully-operational Squabble Cubicle expected shortly, and rumour has it that a Vorgolude is on the way.

Decorative Borders

This festive scheme features an Advanced Technology Floral Basket Deterrence System pioneered by Vegetal Security Services. Acknowledgement must also be made to the School of Ornamental Glasswork for their help with walltop decoration.

A Woodland Picnic Site

This handsome Rural Ingestion Leisure Facility is the winning design in a recent competition sponsored by Interglobal Amenities. The judges were particularly impressed by the resourceful and imaginative use of existing components.

Crazy Paving

Decorative paving can be a handy way of using up surplus building material. But beware — the cracks between the slabs can be a haven for all sorts of pests (see page 72, Winkling Procedures).

New Continental Shelves

Fitted Continental Shelves will add style to any undersea *milieu*, and provide useful storage for all those little treasures. Alternatively, there are many kinds of roomy Abyssal Cabinets available.

A Snowflake Clinic

All snowflakes are to conform with Registered Snowflake Design No. 65537f [mid-grey]. Non-conforming snowflakes will undergo corrective treatment in individual grime cubicles before proceeding to the Pattern Equalizing Room.

A Luxury Kiosk

Keyholders must leave the Kiosk in the condition they found it, and are responsible for any damage to the plog awnings or particle drive wheels. Keys to be handed in to the District Kiosk Beadle on departure.

A Concrete Block

The weight of Jupiter, bulk for bulk, is equal to that of ebony. The weight of Saturn is equal to that of deal. The weight of the Earth is equal to that of liquid concrete.

Arctic Draught Excluding

Chilly winds blowing round your Polar Caps can be very uncomfortable on winter nights. This draughtproofing scheme can be installed in a matter of minutes and is fully endorsed by the Federation of Thermal Tundrologists.

113

Coniferous Viaducts

This is the largest coniferous viaduct so far constructed, and has standing room for a total of 1,556 coniferous trees.

A Cloud Latrine

Leaky clouds must be trained to use the Cloud Latrine, which should be sited in a well-ventilated, secluded position. Loitering is expressly forbidden in the Latrine, as is Unlawful Scudding.

Mountain Clocks

These clocks are waterproof and anti-magnetic and accurate to one hundred millionth of a second. They were awarded the Certificate of Meritorious Decency last year by the Guild of Summit Clockwinders and Cairnmen.

Neat Universe Edges

This scheme requires 16.35^{78} million Official Size 2 Waste Receptacles, 16.35^{78} million Authorized 4-Seat Benches, 23.25^{37} million 250 watt Registered Dayglow Light Bulbs, and 10.64^{28} million tons Licensed Grade A Potting Compost.

APPENDICES

The Spoiling Cabinet

Experiment daily with the contents of your Spoiling Cabinet. New powders and lubricants appear regularly, and it is a sad Handyman who does not find pleasure experimenting with them. Here is a list of items which will be found suitable for a basic Cabinet:

Selected Oils and Drawing Creams
'Universal' Spoiling Powders 1-9
mixing bowl and 4ft nozzle spoon
assorted fluming irons
pieces of white cardboard
chafing rods 1-5
Plodium Green 6" Staining Floss
withering agents
3 steeple-latched Brontoploons
2 left-hand Vuple Feeders
gap-toothed Prap and Sprankle
box of 50mm pre-greased Crotoplates
box of 40% bone-trained Silt Hatches
several scanned tri-glass polynodules
pre-timed lichen tweezers
15° plog-sided threggleplivit
5" impervious bladderstrap
20kz Ordnopifflious Protrunary Grapelian
4 bloat-rendered suckering irons
crystals of Fluzopiltric Acid
various abrasive papers
good solid floggle tongs

Permissible Stenching Frequencies

We are fortunate to have a highly developed Stench Broadcasting Network. The following information about frequencies is provided by the Bureau of Stench Cultivation and Control.

frequency	station	time
1175–1398 pwz	Trans-Global Effluviums	12.00am–12.00pm
1399–1477 pwz	Interstink Megaservices	12.00am–12.00pm
1478–1632 pwz	National Noxious	12.00am–12.00pm
1633–1707 pwz	U.N.I.P.O.N.G.	12.00am–12.00pm
1708–1997 pwz	Independent Emissions	12.00am–12.00pm
1998–1999 pwz	The Honeysuckle Channel	03.00am–03.05am

NOTE

For really effective Emanation over the widest possible area, it is advisable to locate your Receiver in a high position relative to the surrounding Countryside.

Recipe for Successful Liverworting

This recipe has been generously contributed by members of MOSS (Movement for the Obliteration of Spore-producing Subversives).

7oz packet frozen puff pastry
6 eggs, beaten
2 cups phlebefrotic doodle-balls, mashed
1 bonespoon Fluzopiltric crystals, blended
   with a little stable juice
3 or 4 drope nuggets, cut in wedges
16 tons rabulated Grodding Loam
7 pre-skinned vermin brains
pinch of mixed hormones

Whip up the mixture on your pelter-board into a stiff paste or flunt. Then dot the surface of the Countryside decoratively with it using a spadging knife. This has an agreeably contaminative effect on any liverworts in the vicinity.

Modern Bonkinology

The following is an abbreviated version of the Vono E. Nebevol Lecture delivered to the Annual Conference on Contemporary Balderdashing by Ork. T. Squodery, Director of the Institute of Bonkin Research.

'Embelen driand nay bodring zwoll. Pleck mi dotrian, swog mi ziplian. Wille yem ma-goshrian! Wille yem zwop fulle ma-goshrian! Esto se pilficitration, lo nobrion zeldered. Plobo quedge welly in Dept 33 (ork blane-crobe nit) en led redderplest grol-plubriand. Prel in ecrimulious dipribulation — nobular Pluzohost, flubinatory Atemplinticle! Wug plef mi-hooligrane? Zug plef ti-vimlicant? Meg trane di bebble-plotty? Norg. Megge rud zi vuple bleen. Welda ma dotrian. Egplo zot wrinard ma thlof grol-piltriand:

1. Prel zulian ne popperclap.
2. Prel neg ork ti-belpitation.
3. Haut agripustule zodiab,
   ne roondaum denderplest.

Himeldy bagproud voondrains! Hog mi tro ecrimant, me wegawul progathonk.'

FLORAL DISOBEDIENCE NOTIFICATION
FORM 73256D [Daisies]

Floral Unit ⎍⎍⎍⎍⎍⎍⎍⎍⎍⎍⎍ was observed in sector (number) .... division .... in the District of .... at .... hours on the .... day of .... this year .... in circumstances giving me reasonable cause to believe that an infringement or infringements (give full details overleaf) was being or had been committed in contravention of the regulations set out in Clauses 92-116 of the Floral Disobedience Act Section 42b (Lower Greeneries, Unlawful Disposition Thereof). I hereby declare that this information is correct.

Number ....

Mark ....

Date ....

For Office Use Only				
Inflictionary level imposed [in Ngs]	9.6	12.1	73	16,003

NOTES

This is one of a number of forms prepared by the Greenery Office to be used under conditions of the utmost secrecy for notifying the Authorities of any infringement or infringements of the Laws of Natural Order and Decency.

It is your solemn and binding duty to report immediately any such infringement or infringements as you may observe among the licensed planetary units in your jurisdiction. Failure to do so will result in the severest penalties.

Other forms may be obtained from the Visiting Prefect, to whom you should return this form when completed. Use block capitals.

OFFICIAL SMOG COUPONS

This page is to be used only for the collection of Official Smog Coupons. Coupons are obtainable only on application to the Ministry of Smogs, using Form S960023/b, which should be completed in full and taken for stamping to the office of a Regional Smog Bailiff. Smog Coupons are not transferable.

AFFIX COUPON HERE	AFFIX COUPON HERE	AFFIX COUPON HERE	AFFIX COUPON HERE
AFFIX COUPON HERE	AFFIX COUPON HERE	AFFIX COUPON HERE	AFFIX COUPON HERE
AFFIX COUPON HERE	AFFIX COUPON HERE	AFFIX COUPON HERE	AFFIX COUPON HERE

Violation of any of the conditions and regulations set out on the reverse of Smog Coupons is an offence carrying a minimum penalty of 25.3kz units of Level 2 Protrunary Compression with an additional discretionary imposition of up to 5.6kz.

KEEP THESE COUPONS IN A SAFE PLACE

ORDER THROUGH VIGILANCE
DECENCY THROUGH PURIFICATION